Original title:

Silent Frost, Shivering Stars

Author: Rosalie Bradford
ISBN HARDBACK: 978-9916-94-522-3
ISBN PAPERBACK: 978-9916-94-523-0

The Chill of Giggles

In winter's grip, the trees wear white,
While squirrels dance, oh what a sight!
They scamper quick, their cheeks puffed wide,
Gathering snacks with frosty pride.

The moonlight beams on snickering fawns,
Who trip on ice in their funny yawns.
They giggle loud, as they try to flee,
Chasing tails, oh so comically.

The snowman’s got a carrot nose,
But sneezes come from frosty clothes.
With buttons shifting left and right,
He wears a scarf that’s quite a sight!

A penguin slips, and then it quacks,
While rabbits jump to clear the tracks.
They tumble down, all in good cheer,
As winter whispers, “Laugh, my dear!”

So let the cold bring jests anew,
With every snowflake’s laugh, it’s true.
Embrace the chill with giggles bright,
For in this frost, joy takes flight!

A Night's Embrace in the Grasp of Ice

The moon wore a coat, oh so bright,
As chilly breezes found their flight.
Snowmen danced with silly glee,
While penguins ordered hot tea.

Icicles hung like crystal spears,
The squirrels borrowed winter gears.
A snowball fight erupted fast,
Who knew that laughter would outlast?

The Glint of Stars in Earthly Chill

Twinkling gems in the blackened skies,
Are they stars or just curious pies?
Frosty air and snickers abound,
As chilly giggles turn around.

Fluffy mittens lost in the snow,
A runaway hat, take it slow!
Snowflakes giggle and tickle your nose,
While ice skates trip on toes that froze.

Ashes of Light in a Frozen Realm

In a land where giggles freeze,
And snowflakes play just as they please.
Fireplaces crackle with a grin,
Roasting marshmallows on a whim.

Winter coats with pockets wide,
Hide secret snacks for the frosty ride.
Beneath a blanket, we share a glare,
As cocoa spills into thin air.

The Breath of Winter's Lament

As winter moans with icy flair,
The rabbit hops without a care.
Chasing snowflakes, oh what a sight,
A frosty face, but spirits bright!

Laughter echoes through the night,
In playful games, we take flight.
While chilly air makes noses red,
We warm our hearts with jokes instead.

Subtle Shimmers of the Night

The moon wore a goofy grin,
As fireflies danced, all dressed in tin.
A squirrel complained, 'It's too cold to play!'
While a cat did a jig, 'I must sway!'

Stars giggled softly, hiding from sight,
They whispered tales of a snowball fight.
The trees, all shivering, shook with glee,
As the wind chuckled, 'Come dance with me!'

Crystalline Dreams in a Starlit Stillness

Beneath the blanket of icy dreams,
A penguin slipped, or so it seems.
With a flap and a flop, it made quite a show,
Hoping for applause from the crowd below.

A snowman sneezed, 'Ah-choo!' in surprise,
While nearby a rabbit rolled its eyes.
'Chill out,' it said, 'We’ll warm up with tea!'
But the snowman replied, 'Just frosty like me!'

Frosted Mirages under Celestial Gaze

A moose donned a scarf, oh-so-chic,
Stumbled right over a snow-covered peak.
And while it wobbled, a crow stole its hat,
'Not cool,' moaned the moose, 'that’s just plain flat.'

The stars above twinkled, a dazzling spree,
Chuckling at antics, wild and free.
A snowflake fell, landed on a toe,
'Hi there!' it said, 'Ready for a snow show?'

Echoing Stars in a Hushed Horizon

The clouds played hide and seek, what a sight,
While a fox tried to catch a shoelace in flight.
An owl hooted, 'What is this mess?'
As the fox tangled, 'Just trying to impress!'

Echoes of laughter bounced through the night,
With each snowy bounce, a new giggly light.
They rolled and they tumbled, in gleeful repose,
In a blanket of laughter, where silliness flows.

The Hushed Palette of Night's Embrace

In the crisp air, socks slide and fall,
Pajamas dance, making no sense at all.
An owl hoots laughter from a nearby tree,
While squirrels plan mischief, oh so carefree.

The moon's a giant pie, with a smile so wide,
It giggles at shadows, trying to hide.
Stars play hopscotch on the frigid ground,
While snowflakes chuckle, without making a sound.

Awakenings Beneath the Icy Dome

Chickens wearing mittens cross the street so bold,
In their feathery outfits, they strut and scold.
The rooster crows, sounding like a trumpet blast,
While rabbits wear earmuffs, wondering how long it'll last.

Icicles dangle like frozen pops on high,
A seal’s belly flops, destined to glide by.
Pine trees in snowsuits wave at the moon,
At winter's odd ball, life’s a comical tune.

Luminescent Whispers in a Chilling Dark

The stars hum songs, like a jazz band sweet,
With meteors tapping a dancing beat.
A snowman croons, in a hat far too tall,
While a gopher giggles, planning a snowball.

The night sky's a canvas, absurd and bright,
Painted with humor, causing delight.
Comets chase squirrels, racing through the chill,
As the world grins wide on this frosty hill.

The Stillness Where Stars Asleep

In the corners of dreams, where oddities loom,
Bunnies wear slippers, shaking off doom.
While fish in warm waters chuckle with glee,
They mock the cold, as if they're so free.

The crayons at rest laugh at the night,
Plotting to color the darkness just right.
And all the tops spin, with giggles and grace,
Creating a ruckus in this quiet place.

Chill Beneath the Celestial Veil

In a world where penguins dance,
They slip on ice, a goofy chance.
With every glide, they tumble down,
Wearing their best frosted crown.

Stars chuckle softly in the night,
As snowflakes twirl in chilly flight.
Squirrels wear scarves, looking for flair,
Chasing their tails in frosty air.

The moon winks at the frosty ground,
Where rabbits hop and giggle around.
Each breath visible, a cloud of dreams,
As giggles echo with winter's schemes.

Beneath this ice, a chuckle grows,
With frosty antics, everyone knows.
So bring your warmth, your hugs, your cheer,
Let’s frolic beneath the twilight sphere.

Glimmers of the Glistening Night

Stars sit twinkling on their perch,
While owls croon a lazy lurch.
Bunnies bounce in pajamas bright,
Underneath the shimmering light.

Snowmen sing in voice so grand,
With carrot noses set to stand.
But a breeze comes, they start to sway,
“Is this how we dance?” they pout and play.

Meanwhile, the moon is cracking jokes,
At sleepy bears and hibernating folks.
Giggles spread from tree to tree,
As frosty friends share glee with glee.

So if you gaze up high tonight,
And see the stars in cozy light,
Remember this, you frosty pals,
Even the chill has room for halts and howls.

A Lullaby in Ice and Space

In a cradle made of silver ice,
Dreams float around, oh so nice.
Bears in coats sing soft and low,
To the twinkling stars that put on a show.

Frosty flakes start to tango spun,
As winter critters have so much fun.
They trip and tumble, what a blast,
In a slushy world, their giggles cast.

With each chilly breath, laughter rings,
While penguins sport their tiny blings.
In this vast chilly expanse, we find,
The joy of the night, so sweet and kind.

So drift away to this funny sight,
Where even the cold warms hearts tonight.
And as you close your sleepy eyes,
Let laughter sparkle under starry skies.

Moonlit Frost on Numbed Horizons

At dawn, the horizon yawns wide,
Shivering critters by the slide.
A moose in boots attempts to glide,
While bunnies watch, eyes open wide.

The snowman’s hat goes flying high,
As frosty winds let out a sigh.
With a little hop and a mighty fling,
His carrot nose does a silly swing.

Stars twinkle down at the fuss and fun,
While flakes keep falling, one by one.
Each shimmer’s a giggle, each glint a grin,
In this frosty hoedown, laughs begin.

So join the dance under icy beams,
With whimsical wishes and frosty dreams.
No chill can hold back joy's ascent,
In this wintry world, hilarity's meant.

The Stillness of a Shattered Sky

Up above, the stars are stuck,
In a blanket, all jumbled up.
Twinkling like they lost their way,
Making wishes, asking to play.

A comet trips and spills its drink,
While planets giggle, start to wink.
The moon's just laughing at the mess,
In this cosmic game of dress and guess.

Even the sun is taking notes,
Of this cold dance with cozy coats.
He's planning just a little prank,
To tickle Venus by the flank!

So when you gaze into the night,
Grab a laugh, and hold it tight.
For even stars can have their fun,
In the chill of a frosty run.

Crystals of Time in Frigid Air

Little ice cubes float around,
Pretending that they're really found.
Making castles, just for kicks,
While snowmen laugh at frozen tricks.

A clock is dancing, frozen stiff,
Ticking soft, a frigid riff.
Sipping coffee, oh so chill,
While winter's joy is hard to kill.

Watch the trees wear sparkly hats,
As squirrels skate like acrobats.
Time takes breaks for silly games,
In this frosty land of frames.

What a sight to see them stride,
In a dance they cannot hide.
Crystals sparkle, laughter flows,
In the icy air, who knows?

Starlit Dreams in a Whispering Cold

Underneath a starry quilt,
Dreams are spinning, never tilled.
Frosty whispers, giggles near,
As night wraps you in its gear.

A shooting star just lost a shoe,
Said, "Oh dear, what can I do?"
Wearing socks that mismatch bright,
He twirls around in frosty flight.

Dreamers dance while shadows play,
In socks that slid away today.
With every laugh, the cold recedes,
As warmth appears, and laughter leads.

So close your eyes, let visions soar,
The chilling night is never bore.
For each starbeam is a jest,
In this icy world, we’re truly blessed.

The Hush of Icebound Memories

Chill takes hold, in the quiet night,
When memories dance in soft moonlight.
They tiptoe on the frozen ground,
With giggles, they are mostly found.

Snowflakes gossip, drifting low,
In a waltz of soft, frosty glow.
Old tales told with cheeks aglow,
Beneath the stars, they twist and flow.

A bridge of ice wobbles but holds,
As laughter's warmth, the cold unfolds.
Past moments freeze, but smiles don’t wait,
For frosty fun to tempt their fate.

So gather ‘round, let whispered dreams,
Thaw the night with frozen schemes.
In this hush where memories gleam,
The cold is just a funny dream.

Fragments of Light in Shadowed Silence

In the dark where whispers cling,
A squirrel wears a diamond ring.
He dances with a frozen mouse,
Declaring it his little house.

Yet in the gloom, a giggle swirls,
As snowmen try some fancy twirls.
With carrot noses set askew,
They laugh out loud, just like we do.

The icicles hang like jiggly jests,
Each one a dripping, silly guest.
They drip-drop dance to frosty tunes,
While hooting owls wear clever moons.

So pass the popcorn, hide the cheese,
The frozen folks are here to tease.
In shadows soft, the laughter flows,
Where chilly tales turn into prose.

Stars Weeping in the Winter Night

Underneath the chilly beams,
A cat is chasing freezing dreams.
It trips on paws with frosty flair,
And bumps its nose, a snowy scare.

The twinkling lights above do laugh,
As snowflakes dance and take a bath.
“Why so glum?” the moonlight beams,
“Shake off that frost, it’s time for schemes!”

A comet zips, a laughter spouts,
“Catch me, catch me!” it brightly shouts.
But cold, old stars just roll their eyes,
While giggles ripple through the skies.

Night gives hugs, but with a chill,
As laughing stars blend warmth with thrill.
So let us toast to winter's fun,
Where humor glimmers like the sun.

Chain of Crystals, Softly Bright

The night is draped in icy lace,
While penguins tango in one place.
They slip and slide, a comical scene,
With snowflakes falling, soft and keen.

A hare with shades joins in the spree,
And carves the words, “Look at me!”
The crystals chuckle, keeping tight,
As dance moves spark in moon’s soft light.

With every step, the laughter grows,
As chilly breezes play in throes.
The freezing giggles tease the air,
While frosty partners shimmy—fair!

Yet when the dawn begins to break,
The chains of fun start to quake.
With bright-eyed cheer, they bid adieu,
To freeze the fun till night breaks through.

Flickers of Hope in a Frozen Abyss

In winter’s clutch, a wise old fox,
Wears tiny boots and fuzzy socks.
He struts about with such a flair,
While giggling rabbits stop and stare.

Upon a stump, the frostbirds sing,
While bouncing snowmen do their thing.
“Were we this silly last year's freeze?”
The question echoes with a tease.

The starry nights turn antics bright,
As ice cubes dance to pure delight.
With every shiver in the air,
The winter plays without a care.

So gather round, dear pals, be bold,
In frozen lands where warmth takes hold.
From icy depths, a smile release,
Finding joy in every chilly piece.

When the Night Holds Its Breath

When twilight dons its icy shawl,
Whispers flee as night begins to crawl.
The moon wears a goofy grin,
While stars twirl like they need a spin.

Snowflakes dance with mischief, oh dear!
Pretending they’re little spies, I hear.
They giggle and tumble, slipping around,
As if playing tag without a sound.

Comets slide by, not one to miss,
They wink and say, 'Hey, watch this!'
But with a slip, they start to fall,
And land on Mars, causing a brawl!

While the night holds its breath in a chuckle,
Dreamers bundle tight, with a cuddle.
So here’s to the galactic jest,
As chilly frolics create the best!

Tears of the Cosmos in Winter's Grasp

From up above, the heavens weep,
Little droplets in a cosmic sweep.
They splash on Earth, like playful tots,
Making snowmen out of silly thoughts.

Stars slip and slide, like butter on toast,
Each shining face has a bubbly boast.
'Look at me!' they giggle and roar,
But end up colliding—what a galactic score!

Galactic snot, falling faster than light,
Makes winter's night a comical sight.
With each icy tear, laughter does bloom,
As planets dance in a frosty room.

So grab your cocoa and snuggle in tight,
For cosmic giggles make everything bright.
These frosty tears give a playful cheer,
As laughter echoes throughout the year!

Echoes of Light in a Frostbitten World

In a land where frigid breezes tease,
Laughter sparkles among the trees.
The echoes of joy bounce off snowbanks,
As frosty whispers give cosmic pranks.

Stars knock on doors, like cheeky friends,
Bringing a chill, but the laughter never ends.
They ask, 'Is there room for one more?'
And giggle as mittens tumble to the floor.

The sun plays hide-and-seek with the moon,
Frosty giggles begin to croon.
But their playful game makes the chill accelerate,
As icicles start to mimic their fate.

When laughter reigns in a frostbitten realm,
Silly shadows begin to overwhelm.
So lift your mug and give a loud cheer,
For the echoes of light make the cold disappear!

Frosted Wishes on a Cosmic Breeze

A barrage of wishes rides on the frost,
As dreams take flight, never feeling lost.
They swirl and twirl in the crisp night air,
Giggling with joy—a frosty affair.

A snowball fight erupts, all for fun,
Stars consume snacks, jittery and spun.
With a flash of light and a puff of smoke,
They burst out laughing at each silly joke.

Snowmen surf on cosmic waves,
Living it up while the universe braves.
Oh, what a sight, with merriment brewed,
Frosted wishes, with cheer, are renewed!

So toast to the chill and frosty delights,
With comets and giggles on wintry nights.
For in every flake, laughter is found,
Whirling through space, in joy, we're unbound!

Chilled Whispers of Night's Embrace

The moon wears a frosty crown,
Snowflakes dance in a goofy gown.
A bear in pajamas, quite a sight,
Sipping cocoa, oh what a night!

Icicles hang from the eaves above,
While squirrels debate a game of shove.
One slips and lands with a comedic thud,
Creating a soft, fluffy, icy stud!

Laughter erupts in the crisp, cool air,
As snowmen gossip, without a care.
They trade frozen jokes, oh what a thrill,
While stars twinkle, a delightful chill!

Chuckle and giggle in the frosty glow,
As the world's winter wonderland begins to show.
With each chilly whisper, the jokes take flight,
In the embrace of this whimsical night!

Starlight's Touch on Icy Ground

A penguin wearing a bowtie struts,
Sliding on ice, oh how it cuts!
Stars above laugh at the silly scene,
As snowflakes swirl like a frosty queen.

A reindeer attempts a ballet dance,
But slips and lands; oh what a chance!
The twinkling stars chuckle with glee,
As winter blankets the old pine tree.

Snowmen boast of their frosty art,
While a squirrel claims he can outsmart!
He builds a tower of snow, up so high,
Only to watch it all collapse, oh my!

Under blankets of white, the world looks bright,
With laughter echoing through the magical night.
Every star shines in delighted cheer,
As winter's humor draws us near!

A Canvas of Stars on Frigid Wings

A fox dressed as a chef flips some pies,
The stars above twinkle with surprise.
As snowflakes fall like glitter from space,
Creating a laugh on each frozen face.

Jokes are exchanged by the frosty breeze,
While a wise old owl munches on peas.
He hoots belly laughs, making heartbeats race,
In the canvas of ice, a comical place.

Bears play charades with icicles near,
One says ‘sledge!’ and the laughter is clear.
As penguins join in with their waddle and sway,
Making funny faces, no serious play!

With starlit smiles, the night feels alive,
As the frosty air makes the laughter thrive.
In this artwork of winter, joy does unfold,
Each moment a story, comically told!

The Hush of Winter's Serenade

The night wears a cloak of frosty fun,
As snowmen racquetball, just begun!
One takes a hit, his carrot nose flies,
While laughter erupts under starry skies.

A dachshund in boots tries to run,
Slipping and sliding, oh so much fun!
The stars giggle, twinkling so bright,
Watching the chaos of this wintry night.

The chilly air carries a faint, soft song,
As frosty critters join, singing along.
Little voices blend in laughter and cheer,
Painting the sky with their warmth so near.

In this hush, the winter plays,
With whimsical antics and silly displays.
Stars wink knowingly, enjoying the spree,
In the magic of winter, so wild and free!

Footprints in the Snowy Stardust

In the night where twinkles play,
My feet dance in a clumsy way.
Each step a slip, a frosty tease,
I'm the star of this winter breeze.

The snowflakes giggle as I glide,
With every leap, my joy can't hide.
I leave my mark, a wacky trail,
A cosmic clown on a frozen sail.

Silly shapes of snowflakes fall,
I look like I'm having a ball!
A snowman sighs, "What a sight!"
Laughing at my starry flight.

As I whirl and twirl in this space,
I'm a joking comet in goofy grace.
With each turn, I shout with glee,
"Who knew winter could be so free?"

When the Sky Holds Its Chill

Beneath a blanket thick and pale,
I shiver like a curious snail.
The air is crisp, my nose a glow,
But laughter's warm, so off I go!

The moon winks bright with chilly wit,
A frosty dance, I won't quit.
I slip and slide on glitter's sheen,
This dance-off is fit for a queen!

Stars play peek-a-boo with the dark,
As I jump, giving snow a spark.
It's a frosty circus, oh what fun!
I trip on my boots, can't even run!

So here I prance, a winter clown,
With laughter echoing all around.
When skies are cold, just bring your cheer,
And turn those shivers into jeers!

Tapestry of Stars and Frosted Night

A canvas bright, with stars to see,
I toss snowballs, so spiritedly!
The night grins wide, a playful spark,
As I cascade, just like a lark.

Each twinkle whispers silly spells,
A frozen dance, it surely gels.
I take a bow for all the snows,
While giggling snowflakes form my clothes.

I trip and tumble, oh what a sight,
My frosty jig beneath the light.
The constellations laugh so bright,
As I twirl in this frosted flight.

With starshine glimmering in my hair,
I'm the giggling ruler of winter's fair.
Each frosty breath a silly tune,
Under the watchful eye of the moon!

In the Grasp of a Frozen Dream

In sketches drawn by nippy breath,
I challenge winter, I'll cheat death!
The stars above toss jokes my way,
While I frolic and jest, come what may.

I make a snowman, tall and grand,
With a snazzy hat and a dancing hand.
He looks confused but joins the laugh,
Together we prance, a silly half.

A frozen grin on my red nose glows,
As chilly breezes make silly shows.
With every twirl, I can't help but beam,
Lost in the laughter, a frozen dream.

The stars clap with delight and cheer,
As I boogie my way without any fear.
Winter's grip can't hold me tight,
For in joy, I find my starry flight!

The Muffled Breath of a Frozen World

In a land where shivers prance,
Snowflakes waltz, they're in a trance.
Penguins wear their knitted hats,
While squirrels skate on skates with spats.

Winds whisper secrets, oh so sly,
They tease kids who forget to tie.
Snowmen boasting, puffed up wide,
Muffin tops they cannot hide.

Chilly critters throw a ball,
Hedgehogs tumble, laughing, fall.
Their tiny paws just cannot grip,
On icy patches, they do slip.

Frosty giggles fill the air,
Winter’s jokes, beyond compare.
A frozen world, so full of cheer,
With icy chuckles, we persevere.

Distant Glimmers in the Quiet Dark

Stars are sneezing, what a sight,
Twinkling jokes in the twilight.
A comet's tail, a puppy's wag,
In the dark, they play and brag.

Moon's a lantern, so confused,
As the planets laugh, bemused.
Saturn wears a ring of pie,
Jupiter's spotted—oh my, oh my!

While meteors do a quick dance,
Falling fast, they take a chance.
And all the owls roll their eyes,
"Seriously, guys? What a surprise!"

Galaxies spin in a playful race,
Cosmic humor fills the space.
With each wink and shimmering flute,
Even the universe finds its loot.

Icy Breath of the Sleeping Cosmos

The stars gather for a night-time feast,
Jupiter's bringing his cheeky yeast.
Mars tries to tell a frosty joke,
But Venus just giggles, nearly choked.

Chilly laughter echoes bright,
As snowy comets take their flight.
Asteroids wobble, dance, and sway,
While Saturn's rings just mock their play.

Pluto rolls by, a tiny guy,
With a frosty grin, oh my, oh my!
He trips on a crater, lands with flair,
Throwing stardust all through the air.

A whispering breeze, an icy sigh,
From worlds that twinkle up high.
With every chuckle from afar,
The cosmos spins, a winking star.

A Page of Frost Beneath the Stars

In the night, the ground is white,
Frogs in mittens, a silly sight.
They hop along on frosty toes,
As snowflakes tickle their chilly noses.

A curious fox in a velvet coat,
Writes in snow, his little note.
"Hey winter, can you be less bold?
I'd like some sunshine, not so cold!"

Underneath skies that blush and glow,
Bears are snuggled, wrapped in snow.
While bunnies play hopscotch on ice,
With carrots armed, they roll them nice.

Stars all twinkle with laughter sweet,
As nature's mischief fills the street.
With a page of frost, dreams are spun,
Even the cold can be such fun!

Breath of the Aurora in Distant Light

A chilly breeze, wearing a coat,
Whispers to penguins on a drifting boat.
They laugh at the ice, all sparkly and bright,
While dancing around like it’s ball night!

Snowflakes tease with a dainty swirl,
As snowmen complain, 'Do I really twirl?'
With carrot noses that giggle and shake,
In the frosty air, they just can’t take.

Twinkling lights in the sky engage,
Frosty jokes play out on this grand stage.
The stars wink back in a gleeful jest,
Even the moon can't help but just rest.

So let’s raise our mugs, filled with hot cocoa,
Toast to the ice-queen and her igloo’s glow.
With laughter and warmth, we’ll forget the chill,
And dance in the dark, with a whimsical thrill.

The Still Mind of a Frozen Universe

In the vast expanse, where thoughts take flight,
A brain freeze occurs in the dead of night.
With icy ideas that tingle and tease,
Even the snowmen can’t catch a breeze!

Stars gather 'round for a comedy show,
As comets crack jokes, making stardust glow.
But if you listen close, beneath all the fun,
You’ll hear a chill chuckle from Saturn's sun.

Galaxies stretch, feeling quite vast,
But they’re tangled up like a braid too fast.
While planets weigh in with their weighty tales,
They slip on the ice and it always fails!

Yet in this stillness, a laughter may spark,
Like winter’s embrace, bringing cheer to the dark.
So dance with the frost, let your spirit soar,
In this frozen realm, we’re never a bore.

When the Wind Whispers Secrets of Ice

The wind bends low with gossip so crisp,
Secretly sharing with every eavesdropper's lisp.
It tells of the snowflakes, their secrets to keep,
While yetis roll by in a whirl of sleep.

Oh, how the shadows giggle and sway,
As icicles laugh at the bright sun's rays.
Each gust brings a chuckle, a playful tease,
'Who slipped on the ice?' asks the nearby trees.

But don't mind the frost, it's here to amuse,
With its chilly banter, it's sure to confuse.
It pulls on our scarves with a mischievous hand,
Inviting us all to join in its band.

So bundled up tight, let's frolic and laugh,
At adventures that dance on this icy path.
For in every breeze, a jest can be found,
The wind hums a tune, a cheerful sound.

Shimmers of Hope in the Void

In the black of night, a spark lights the way,
Dressed in frost, stars begin to play.
They twinkle and wink from their lofty perch,
With a wink and a giggle, they give us a lurch.

A comet zooms by with a vibrant cheer,
Yelling, 'Don’t freeze, come dance with your peers!'
A parade of planets joins in the fray,
While moons roll their eyes at the silliness sway.

Hope shimmers lightly, like ice on a lake,
Though we stumble and trample, no hearts will break.
With branches like dancers, they sway to the breeze,
Nature’s own party, urging us to tease.

So as the stars shine with frost that's no curse,
We’ll laugh and we’ll giggle, for better or worse.
In this cosmic jest, let’s all play our part,
For giggles and sparkles warm every heart.

The Sigh of Stars Under Winter's Gaze

In the night, the stars do sneeze,
Wrapped in blankets, feeling the breeze.
They twinkle under a frosty mug,
Wishing for cocoa, all snug as a bug.

Snowflakes giggle, down they glide,
Wondering if the moon can slide.
Comets dance in a chilly waltz,
Making snowmen with bounce and vaults.

The chilly air hums a jolly tune,
While clouds play peek-a-boo with the moon.
Stars are counting the flakes that fall,
Each one a wish, a silly call.

"Hey look! An igloo!" one star cries out,
"Or is it a penguin in a cozy spout?"
Across the sky, laughter does soar,
With each twinkling giggle, we want more!

Shadows of Dreams in Frozen Stillness

Dreams take a stroll in the frozen night,
Wearing scarves made of pure starlight.
They trip on snowflakes, tumble and roll,
Chasing each other, heart and soul.

The moon tells jokes in a frosty voice,
While stardust giggles, it has no choice.
A snowman pulls a carrot nose,
Whispers, "I'm chillin', how about you, bros?"

Chilly shadows do the polka dance,
With icicles swinging, all in a trance.
As stars throw snowballs, both bright and wild,
Even the universe can act like a child.

"Hey look, a dream!" one whispers aloud,
"It's wearing pajamas, it's cozy and proud!"
Wishes swirl in the frosty air,
With giggles and chuckles, joys we all share.

Sparkling Silence of Outer Realms

In vast realms where the cool winds swirl,
Stars don’t just shine, they twirl and whirl.
Floating around on ice cream cones,
Making wacky shapes with rolling stones.

Galaxies grab their coats, so bright,
Riding bicycles made of cookie dough light.
Every glimmer a slip and slide,
Where comets race on a sugar ride.

“Who’s making snow angels?” one star gabs,
“Not me, I rather eat fluffs of jabs!”
Floating in joy, balloons in the tail,
Jingle-bells echo through starlit gale.

With winks and flickers, the cosmos plays,
Dancing to rhythms of candy cane ways.
In this chilly circus, laughter unfurls,
Through the sparkling silence of all the worlds.

Celestial Frost and the Dance of Night

In chilly realms where bright lights gleam,
Stars prepare for a dazzling dream.
They don their hats, all sparkly and bright,
Ready to waltz through the crisp, cool night.

Frosty thoughts on a comet's tail,
Make snowflakes giggle with a tickly trail.
While galaxies spin their whimsical yarns,
Creating the quirkiest celestial barns.

“Is that a shooting star or a falling fry?”
One star yells out with a twinkly sigh.
They chuckle and laugh, like friends at a show,
“Who knew the night was this fun to throw?”

So join the dance, let your heart take flight,
In the chilly embrace of the wondrous night.
For in this great cosmos, we play, sing and beam,
With laughter and joy in an endless dream.

Nightfall's Gentle Caress

The moon wears a smile, oh so bright,
While critters hold a disco at night.
Stars gossip softly, plotting their fun,
While shadows do the cha-cha, one by one.

The chill in the air gives a ticklish tease,
As squirrels in sweaters sip on some breeze.
They twirl and they whirl, in this frosty land,
With icicles tapping, putting on a band.

Sudden slips on frost, what a sight it makes,
As penguins on ice throw hilarious shakes.
Laughter erupts like the bubbles in tea,
In this quirky dance of cosmic glee.

So if you see a comet trip in the sky,
Know it's just a ballerina, oh me, oh my!
Nightfall's embrace, a whimsical show,
With giggles galore, and a fuzzy glow.

The Breath of the Universe in Stillness

Whispers of cosmos, tea time in space,
With aliens sipping on saucers, what grace!
They offer us cookies from faraway lands,
While comets juggle with sparkly bands.

A chilly breeze sends warm laughs awhirl,
As stardust confetti gives planets a twirl.
Nebulae snicker at creatures who freeze,
In helmets too tight, wheezing, 'Oh please!'

Galactic puns float on the tip of the night,
Like 'Why don’t stars ever get into a fight?'
'Cause they always seem to shine and not whine,
Comic relief in the vast by design!

So as we float in this sparkling stew,
With laughter like magic, our hearts feel anew.
In stillness we find, a funny embrace,
The universe giggles, a cheerful space.

Icy Veils Draped Over Twilight

Twilight arrives, dressed in layers of fun,
As snowflakes begin their dance—look, they run!
Penguins wear tuxedos, ready to play,
While the owls in shades supervise the ballet.

Frosty whispers tingle on cheeks like a jest,
As squirrels throw snowballs, they think they're the best.
A turtle, confused, stumbles into a fig,
While rabbits in mittens teach others to dig!

Even the moon tries to catch a cold,
With blankets of winter, fetching but bold.
While the stars are pursuing a snowball fight,
Oh what a picture, a whimsical sight!

With laughter layered thick like the snow,
The twilight reflects all the warmth in its glow.
So when icy veils wrap the world all around,
Let your chuckles echo, let joy abound.

Frost-Kissed Echoes of Distant Worlds

In realms far away where the giggles abound,
Frost-kissed echoes make a hilarious sound.
Planets collide in a ticklish embrace,
While aliens laugh, sharing jokes at their place.

A nebula hiccups, with stardust delight,
Creating a scene that sparks laughter so bright.
With twinkly eyes, they send jokes through the air,
Like, 'What did the comet say? Just trust the flare!'

For even in silence, a chuckle will spread,
As asteroids play hopscotch—imagine the spread!
Galaxies chat, sharing frosty pizza pies,
While the sun gently sighs, rolling its eyes.

So let’s lift our voices to the chill of the night,
With frosty tales waiting for laughter's delight.
In echoes of starlight, the humor resounds,
In this cosmic dance, joy always abounds.

The Frigid Silence Between the Stars

In the night, the moon does freeze,
While owls laugh with frosty knees.
Stars play hide and seek with light,
Sipping cocoa, out of sight.

Snowflakes waltz with cheeky grins,
They tumble down like playful sins.
Giggling winds in chilly tunes,
They tickle trees under the moons.

A Serene Canvas of Glacial Light.

The canvas glows with icy charms,
While penguins arm-wrestle in farms.
Snowmen boast of carrot fights,
While sleds take off at dizzy heights.

Beneath the chill, the rabbits scoff,
As they watch their friends just fall off.
Chasing shadows without a care,
Hopping ‘round in the frosty air.

Whispers of Winter's Embrace

Whispers travel through frozen pines,
As squirrels debate their fashion lines.
In coats of white, they strut and spin,
While chilly winds just grin and win.

The snowball fights have quite the flair,
As brothers tumble without a care.
The laughter echoes through the night,
Lit by stars that twinkle bright.

Dances of Frozen Light

In icy boots, the children glide,
Trying hard not to collide.
With giggles bright and cheeks aglow,
They pirouette like pro ballet foes.

The frosty paths are full of cheer,
With snowmen winking, drawing near.
Each twirl and jump brings hearty laughs,
As winter plays its playful paths.

Beneath the Frost, the Heartbeats Stir

The chilly air makes noses red,
And penguins slip on ice, oh dread!
While hearts beneath the snow do dance,
In winter coats, we prance and prance.

With mittens bright and socks that clump,
We do the frosty shuffle, bump!
Our laughter echoes in the freeze,
As snowflakes tickle, twist, and tease.

Hot cocoa mustache, quite the sight,
Makes sliding down the hill feel right.
We tumble down, a giggling mess,
Oh, winter fun, we must confess!

Yet as we thaw beneath the sun,
We'll laugh at all the frozen fun.
With hearts so warm and cheeks aglow,
We'll chase the chills, with joy we sow.

Still Waters of the Eternal Night

The stars above begin to wink,
As moonlight makes the ice rink stink.
We glide and slip, a clumsy crew,
With fancy moves that feel brand new.

The fish beneath just roll their eyes,
As we make leaps that weren't so wise.
They whisper, "What a silly bunch,
Kick, slide, then take the nightly plunge!"

But laughter fills the frozen air,
As we pretend we have no care.
In twinkling lights, our shadows dance,
While frozen toes lead us to chance.

In stillness rare, we share a laugh,
As ice turns into a chilly path.
We joke with stars, a light-hearted spree,
What’s the frost without this glee?

The Echo of Stars in a Frigid Breeze

A chilly breeze whispers a jest,
Where snowflakes play their very best.
They spiral down like little hats,
Then stick to noses, oh, such spats!

The stars above twinkle in glee,
As we chase shadows by the tree.
“Look! There’s a comet!” we yell out,
But it’s just a squirrel — roundabout!

With every slip, we share a cheer,
Making memories full of frosty cheer.
And if we fall, well, what a sight,
Rolling in laughter ‘til late at night.

So here we craft our cosmic play,
In chilly air, we’ll laugh and sway.
For every slip and every flinch,
Transforms into joy — not a pinch!

Frosted Whispers in Cosmic Lullabies

Beneath the skies where frost holds sway,
We dance in dreams till break of day.
With snowmen grinning, all a-smile,
We join the fun, let's stay awhile!

In nightly whispers, the stars conspire,
Their twinkling light we all admire.
But watch your step, oh, fate beware,
As icy tiles may lead to flair!

With giggles echoing through the night,
A snowball fight brings such delight.
Till cheeks are flushed and spirits soar,
We roll and laugh, we chase for more.

At dawn's first light, as frost induces,
We see our prints, the funny muses.
And when we smile at tales we weave,
Frosty magic makes us believe.

Frosted Dreams on a Still Canvas

In the morn, the laughter's cold,
Jokes to tell, they never get old.
Snowmen grin with carrot noses,
While penguins dance in frosty poses.

Hot cocoa spills on winter's spree,
But marshmallows float, carefree,
Socks slide on the icy floor,
A slip, a fall—who could ask for more?

Blankets piled, a fort is made,
Imagination, unafraid.
Chasing snowflakes with a cheer,
“Catch me if you can!” we jeer.

The sun peeks through with a subtle grin,
But back to the chill, we’re ready to spin.
With dreams so frosty all around,
Laughter echoes, and joy is found.

Nightfall's Chilling Embrace

When twilight falls, the giggles rise,
Moonlight dances with boundless eyes.
Hats and scarves in disarray,
Time for snowball fights at play!

Icicles hang like toothy grins,
Laughter rings as the dusk begins.
Fingers cold, but hearts burn bright,
'Til we can't tell day from night.

The stars peer down, curious in glee,
Watching friends, wild and free.
Sneezes echo, a frosty sneeze,
And hot tea spills with an icy breeze.

Under blankets, stories are spun,
Of brave knights and dragons that run.
A tickle and giggle chase the chill,
As winter nights stretch, time stands still.

Glimmering Tales in the Dark

In the dark, the shadows creep,
Monsters hide beneath our sleep.
But wait! What's that? A squeaky mouse,
With a hat, he takes a bow in the house.

While children dream of sugar plums,
Snowflakes swirl like tiny drums.
The stars above begin to chatter,
"Who knew cold could make such a patter?"

Puffer jackets waddling near,
As snowflakes fall, they disappear.
Laughter rings like distant bells,
In the frosty air, our joy swells.

A snowman's hat flew right away,
Chasing it feels like child's play.
Silly faces, icy grins,
In the dark, the fun begins!

A Shroud of Stillness Overhead

Stars above shine bright and clear,
As we cherish winter's cheer.
With shivers come hilarious pranks,
Frosty laughs fill the cold, icy banks.

Sledding down the hills with style,
In the air, we spin and smile.
A crash, a laugh, "Oh, what a fall!"
Snow's not sticky, it's a fuzzy ball!

Gloves wet, but spirits high,
Nutty snowmen dancing nearby.
They can't twirl, but they sure can sway,
As we stomp our feet in cheerful dismay.

At night we sit, the chill draws near,
Hot soup and giggles, winter cheer!
With every bite, a chuckle erupts,
Frosty nights fill with giggles unducted.

Whispers of Winter's Breath

The trees wore jackets, all snug and tight,
As squirrels threw snowballs, what a funny sight!
A rabbit slipped, doing a twist and shout,
While penguins laughed, waddled about.

Frosty tongues stuck out, tasting the chill,
Hot cocoa giggles, that warms up the thrill.
Icicles are hanging, like swords from the roof,
Making our noses turn red like a poof!

Starlit Veils of Crystal Night

Stars wearing scarves, shimmering bright,
As comets play tag in the chilly night.
A snowman grinned, with a carrot snout,
While chatting with owls, oh what a clout!

Each flake fell down, like a tiny ballet,
Making snow angels that giggled away.
The moon cracked jokes, with a mischievous wink,
And frost-nipped noses began to rethink!

The Quiet Dance of Ice and Light

Penguins in top hats, a dance on the ice,
Wobbling and juggling, oh, isn’t it nice?
While snowflakes giggle and scatter around,
Catching the giggles that lightly resound.

The shadows were playing a game of freeze,
As ice cubes formed a band, oh what a tease!
With glimmering toes, they stomped through the snow,
While chill-breathing dragons put on a show.

Echoes Beneath a Glistening Sky

Beneath the glowing sky, whispers are found,
As snow dressed the rooftops, covering the ground.
Frosty fingers tickling, making us squeal,
While dripping icicles play “catch me, if real.”

The moon shared secrets, just laugh and behold,
While chilly marmots joined a race, bold.
A penguin slipped over, causing a spree,
With frosty giggles spreading like glee!

Celestial Crystals in Moonlight

Underneath the pale moon glow,
A snowman's laugh begins to flow.
He slips on ice with grace so rare,
And then he tumbles in mid-air.

Stars above point and giggle bright,
As he lands with a puffy light.
His carrot nose starts to protest,
'Why can't I just be like the rest?'

The night brings frost, and oh, what fun!
Shooting stars play tag, one by one.
But off they go with a dazzling dash,
While snowflakes dance in a frosty flash.

So every winter, when stars are awake,
The humor shines in the ice they make.
A sparkling world where laughter’s king,
In this chilly realm, joy takes wing.

Beneath the Veil of Frosted Ethers

In the stillness, something's amiss,
A penguin slips, gives winter a kiss.
With flippers flailing, he takes a spin,
'Why's ice so slippery? Where do I begin?'

Frosty branches creak and crack,
As squirrels plot their sneaky attack.
They gather nuts with a frantic rush,
While giggling at a sleepy hush.

The trees giggle, decked in white,
'Watch your step, you might take flight!'
But they just sway, and the stars above,
Laugh at the chaos, filled with love.

So under the veil of icy mist,
Laughter echoes in a frosty twist.
Nature's joke lasts all night long,
In this whimsical, chilly song.

The Cold Lullaby of Twinkling Lights

Twinkling gems in a sky so clear,
Sneeze a comet, oh what a cheer!
While frosty critters waddle and dance,
Flipping and flopping, they take a chance.

A bunny hops, it boing-boings high,
While snowflakes fall gently from the sky.
They land on noses, a giggly sight,
All bundled up, a cozy delight.

The chill hums softly a frosty tune,
As icicles clink like a rhythmic spoon.
But then a rabbit jumps out of line,
And gets stuck in a snowman’s spine!

The giggles grow, the night’s in glee,
As stars wink down playfully.
In this cold lullaby, jokes abound,
As winter's charm wraps all around.

Shivers Beneath a Silver Dome

Beneath a dome of shimmering white,
Froggy slips, it gives him fright!
With a belly flop, he lands with flair,
'Is winter laughing? I couldn't bear!'

The owls watch with their big, round eyes,
As they hoot softly, plotting surprise.
While on the ground, a clownish hare,
Practices flips with a frosty flair.

Chilly winds sing a wild, fun song,
As the moon hangs out, cheerful and strong.
Under its light, all frolic and play,
With icy giggles leading the way.

In this winter wonder, let's have a laugh,
For funny moments make winter a path.
So gather your friends under this dome,
And dance in the chill, call it home.

A Symphony of Cold and Quiet

Beneath the moon, the snowflakes cheer,
As penguins slide, without a fear.
They waddle and dance, in winter's chill,
Making us laugh, as they take a spill.

The trees are dressed in shimmering white,
And squirrels shout, what a frosty night!
They chatter and prance, with acorn flair,
While snowmen grin, like they just don’t care.

The stars above wear icy crowns,
As polar bears run, slipping around.
They tumble and flip, in the glistening glow,
A chilly circus, put on a show!

So grab your mittens, and join the fun,
In this winter wonder, 'til day is done.
With giggles and chills, let the mischief spread,
Till warm cocoa calls us to cozy our bed.

Glacial Dreams on Starry Pathways

Dreams of snowflakes swirl in the air,
While owls hoot jokes with frosty flair.
A bunny in boots hops right on cue,
Sledding on fluff that’s sparkly blue.

Stars start to giggle, they twinkle and blink,
As they watch the raccoons trying to think.
They steal from the bins and plan a feast,
Shouting, 'No longer are we just a beast!'

Icicles dangle like ornaments bright,
And penguins hold parties each chilly night.
With fish-sushi snacks that they surely crave,
They slide on their bellies, oh what a wave!

So tiptoe softly, and join in their lark,
As frost-covered critters ignite a spark.
In laughter and joy, winter dances around,
With playful antics in the crisp ground.

Infinity Wrapped in a Chilly Hush

In the hush of the night, the squirrels unite,
For a winter soiree, all bundled up tight.
Snowballs are flying with giggles galore,
As the rabbits watch out for a snowman’s war.

The stars form a band, singing songs in the breeze,
While frosty-hued fairies giggle with ease.
They twirl in the dark, with sparkly delight,
Turning the world into a wondrous sight.

Cold toes and warm hearts, a whimsical sight,
As we chase our breath in the frosty night.
Snowmen look smug with their carrot-nosed grins,
While owls offer wisdom on how the fun begins.

So grab your buddy, let’s bundle and run,
Through snowdrifts and starlight, we’ll chase the fun.
With giggles entwined in this frostbitten air,
Let’s dance till the morning – without a care!

The Dance of Twilight in Icy Embrace

Twilight winks, as penguins parade,
In tuxedos of snow, perfectly made.
They slide and they glide on a frosty spree,
Chasing their tails, oh what glee!

The moon whispers softly, 'Don't take a spill!'
But goofy old raccoons, they never stand still.
With a clatter and flurry, they tumble about,
Creating a ruckus, without a doubt.

Meanwhile the stars, like glittering eyes,
Are chuckling at critters beneath the skies.
As frostbitten bunnies hop up for a dance,
Shivering to rhythms of winter’s romance.

So join the fun in this icy embrace,
With laughter and snow, we’ll keep up the pace.
In a world made of giggles, where the cold ends,
We’ll dance through the night, with our fluffy friends.

The Night's Caress of Frozen Fire

In a fluffy blanket, I lay so snug,
My nose turned red like a chilly bug.
Stars wink at me with their glimmering laughs,
While I sip hot cocoa from overfilled calfs.

The moon's a big donut, so sweet and round,
While snowflakes dance paws up from the ground.
A feline in boots slides past with delight,
Guess I'll call it a night — oh wait, what a sight!

My teeth chatter tunes, a jazzy refrain,
Yet nobody listens, they're all wrapped in grain.
A penguin in shorts bids the polar bears cheer,
"Who ordered the cold? It's not summer here!"

So I yawn at the frost, with a giggle so bright,
Living dreams under ribbons of twinkling light.
The stars take a bow, what a comical play,
As I snuggle my blanket and drift far away!

Shimmering Secrets of the Frosty Void

In the backyard, the dog has donned a cape,
He flies through the snow, a merdog escape!
While squirrels in mittens hold tiny tea leaves,
Exchanging their recipes with cheeky reprieves.

The moon throws a party for critters and scamps,
Where rabbits perform as the tap-dancing champs.
Snowmen are judges, with noses of gold,
Scoring high marks for those brave and bold!

Lights twinkle like giggles from heaven above,
Chasing away gloom, filling hearts with love.
Each flake, a puzzle, a riddle untold,
Adds to the laughter, a sight to behold!

So, let's raise our cups, made of frosty dreams,
Sharing secrets and laughter under distant beams.
While mischief abounds in this wintery plot,
Who knew the cold could be this funny a lot?

Twilight's Chill Kisses the Twinkling

Twilight sneezes, a gust of delight,
While shivers dance with the stars in the night.
A cat in a top hat tips tales of the sky,
Chasing the moonbeams that playfully fly.

Yes, owls in spectacles discuss the high news,
Debating if snow is better than shoes.
As ice cubes chime like a grand tea affair,
The daisies are dreaming of summer to share.

They twirl in the frost, those giggling puffs,
While icicles chime like silly old fluffs.
The breeze chuckles low, a belly of cheer,
I'm thankful for cold—though I'd love a warm beer!

Stars laugh and wink, topping smiles all around,
As the world starts spinning with joy, so profound.
Twilight whispers sweet nothings with glee,
In this humorous hush, how cozy we be!

Ethereal Glints on Wistful Nights

Ethereal sparkles dance on the street,
While I chase my cat in her glittery feet.
She trips on a snowdrift, oh what a sight,
Cursing the frost with a flick and a bite.

Winter doves gossip, wearing knitted vests,
Discussing the warmth of their snug, feathered nests.
The trees pipe up with a crackling cheer,
As icicles jingle like bells, oh so near!

With marshmallows flying, a playful spree,
I laugh at the frost that's so goofily free.
The whisper of cold tickles cheeks in delight,
As we bundle up and start frolicking bright.

The stars plot mischief, twinkling afar,
As hot chocolate dreams under a comet's bizarre.
In this frosty embrace, with smiles at the helm,
We laugh at the cold; it's our wondrous realm!

Milton Keynes UK
Ingram Content Group UK Ltd.
UKHW020237211124
451186UK00007BA/148

9 789916 945223